Cornerstones of Freedom

The Story of
THE GOLD
AT SUTTER'S MILL

By R. Conrad Stein

Illustrated by Lou Aronson

CHILDRENS PRESS, CHICAGO

Library of Congress Cataloging in Publication Data

Stein, R. Conrad.
  The story of the gold at Sutter's Mill.

(Cornerstones of freedom)
  Summary: Presents the scene in California after
gold was discovered on John Sutter's land in 1849 and the
subsequent fortunes made and hearts broken.
  1. Sutter's Fort (Sacramento, Calif.)—Juvenile
literature. 2. Sutter, John Augustus, 1803-1880—
Juvenile literature. 3. Sacramento (Calif.)
Fortifications, military installations, etc.—Juvenile
literature. 4. California—Gold discoveries—Juvenile
literature. 5. California—History—1846-1850—
Juvenile literature. |1. California—Gold discoveries|
I. Aronson, Lou. II. Title. III. Series.
F865.S8193   979.4'04   81-6088
ISBN 0-516-04617-9   AACR2

6 7 8 9 10 R 91 90

For thousands of years, streams in central California wound peacefully through the hills. Indians paused at those streams to drink the crystal-clear water. Now and then they saw glints of yellow in the streambeds. They nodded and passed on. The Indians of old California had no use for gold.

Other men, however, were willing to risk their lives for gold. When they learned of the rich deposits in California, they headed west like stampeding cattle.

The great race to California began in 1849. The first traces of gold had been found a year earlier on the property of John Augustus Sutter.

Sutter was an unlikely figure to be remembered in history books. In 1832 he had left his native Switzerland to come to the United States. At the time, he had no money and was escaping his many debts at home. After drifting from state to state, Sutter decided to go to California. He arrived there in 1839.

California then belonged to Mexico. It was a huge area where few people lived. The Mexican settlements amounted to a dozen or so missions that were strung out between the struggling village of Los Angeles and the shores of San Francisco Bay.

Giving away large pieces of land to settlers was common in early California. Sutter talked the governor into giving him 50,000 acres in the rich Sacramento Valley. In the past, he had tried and failed at many different businesses. But with so much land, Sutter believed he could now become as wealthy and powerful as the noblemen he had admired while growing up in Switzerland.

In 1846 war broke out between Mexico and America. Because of that war, California became a territory of the United States.

Sutter paid little attention to the war. A dream churned in his mind. He hoped to acquire still more land and establish his own empire in California. Already he had built a fort near the American River, and now called himself "Captain Sutter."

One day in January, 1848, Sutter's foreman hurried inside Sutter's office and shut the door. Then he showed Sutter two pieces of yellow metal about the size of unpopped popcorn.

Sutter rolled them in his fingers. "Gold?" he asked.

The foreman nodded.

Sutter smiled. Gold on his property would make him even richer and more powerful than he had dared to dream.

Neither Sutter nor his foreman knew they were sitting on top of enough gold to turn sleepy California into a booming territory almost overnight.

At first Sutter tried to keep the discovery a secret, but the news soon leaked out. A ten-year-old boy, a son of Sutter's cook, found a tiny gold lump on the riverbank. He proudly showed it to passersby. One of them was a man who delivered goods by horse and wagon to the scattered farms in the Sacramento Valley. In a few weeks the valley was buzzing with the news that gold had been found at Sutter's Mill.

About a month after the find, a small newspaper called the *Californian* reported:

> GOLD MINE FOUND — In the newly made raceway of the sawmill erected by Captain Sutter on the American fork, gold has been found in considerable quantities.

The newspaper article was incorrect. So far, only a tiny amount of gold had been found. But the mention of gold can bring forth feelings of excitement and greed in the most sensible of men. So the article was read closely by everyone in California.

Those first few specks of gold were the germs of what became a new disease. Gold fever struck at Sutter's Mill and swept through California like an epidemic.

Men dropped what they were doing and rushed to the mill. Farmers left plows in the fields. Store owners bolted their doors shut. Workers put aside their tools.

The newspaper that broke the story had to shut down. The reporters and pressmen ran off to dig for gold. The newspaper's last editorial said:

> The whole country from San Francisco to Los Angeles resounds with the sordid cry of gold! GOLD! GOLD! GOLD! While the field is left half planted, the house half built, and everything neglected but the manufacturers of shovels and pickaxes.

Suddenly everyone in California became a gold miner. And some of them were very lucky. A man

named Joe Dye collected $40,000 in gold in just seven weeks. Two partners, William Daylor and Perry McCoon, made $17,000 in one week. A boy named Davenport, who claimed to be twelve years old but looked even younger, found $2,700 worth of gold in just two days.

As in many other enterprises, the people who were there first got the most. A year later an army of miners descended on California. Then gold mining became hard work. Only a lucky few made quick fortunes.

News of the gold find spread east. Hunters and traders crossing the Great Plains talked to settlers on the Mississippi. They said that in California huge chunks of gold covered the ground like stones. Sailors who had shipped out of San Francisco brought stories of California gold to eastern cities. They told of men in California who had become overnight millionaires. Most of the stories were exaggerated, but they were based on truth.

The gold found at Sutter's Mill caused one of the wildest mass movements of people the world had ever seen—the Great California Gold Rush.

From the farms, small towns, and cities of the eastern United States men headed to California.

Many of them carried washbowls. They hoped to use these to "wash" or "pan" gold out of the sand. A popular song in the East was sung to the tune of "Oh! Susanna!"

Oh! California! That's the land for me!
I'm bound for California with my washbowl on my knee.

In the year 1849, some 85,000 gold seekers swarmed to California. Those early arrivals were called "forty-niners."

Most forty-niners were young men in their teens and early twenties. They were looking for adventure, as well as a fortune. Other forty-niners were older men. Many of them had deserted their families because of the lure of gold.

The first decision a forty-niner faced was how to get to California. He could choose one of three ways. One was to take a ship out of an Atlantic port, sail around Cape Horn at the tip of South America, and then go up the Pacific Coast to San Francisco. A second route was to go overland by horse and wagon or on foot. A third was a combination of the first two—take a ship to Mexico or Panama, cross overland, and then take another ship heading north to California.

The route by sea appealed to men from the East Coast. Sleek new clipper ships were fast, but they mainly carried cargo. So most of the forty-niners who took this route sailed on older, slower ships. It took these ships six or eight months to go from the East Coast to San Francisco. Greedy ship captains took as many passengers as they could cram on board. So in the holds, the gold seekers slept three to a bed. The beds were stacked one on top of the other. They were so close together that the passengers had no room to sit up. The food they were served was a dreadful mixture of salt pork and beans. One forty-niner later wrote that "there were two bugs for every bean." Sometimes the quality of the food didn't matter. Most passengers lost their appetites while rounding Cape Horn. Violent storms there tossed ships about like toy boats in a bathtub. Many forty-niners became so seasick they cursed the day they decided to seek gold.

The most popular route to the gold fields was the one that ran overland. Forty-niners gathered in groups at frontier settlements such as St. Joseph on the Missouri River. From there—by horse, wagon, mule, and on foot—they headed west. They followed almost the same route explorers Lewis and Clark had taken some fifty years earlier. The gold seekers soon encountered Plains Indians, but most Indians wanted only to trade. After passing through the Great Plains, the forty-niners had trouble finding water and grass for their animals. Near the Sierra Nevada Mountains, the travelers faced a hellish stretch of land called the Forty-Mile Desert. One forty-niner wrote to a friend who was about to take the trip, "Expect to find the worst desert you ever saw, and then find it worse than you expected."

Many gold seekers thought the best route to California was the one that ran over both land and water. Most of them crossed overland at Panama. This meant a long trip through mosquito-infested swamps. Dozens of miners caught malaria there and died—still more than a thousand miles from California. To cross Panama, miners hired native boatmen to paddle them through the maze of rivers that cut from one side of the country to the other. The boatmen found that they could charge whatever fee they wished. The price of a passage for two men rose from $10 to $50 in just a few months. The Panamanians liked to sing as they rowed through the jungle rivers. They spoke no English, but because of the forty-niners their favorite songs became "Oh! Susanna!" and "Yankee Doodle."

When he finally arrived in the gold fields, the forty-niner faced shocking prices. A horse that a year before had sold for $6 in California now cost a whopping $300. The price of food was enough to make a miner cry. A loaf of bread—$2. A pound of butter—$6. One egg—$3. A tin of sardines (a treat for the miner)—$16.

At the very start of the gold rush, merchants discovered they could charge miners outrageous prices and get away with it. When gold fever first struck California, a store owner named Sam Brannan learned that iron pans were needed to take gold from streambeds. At twenty cents apiece, Brannan bought practically every iron pan in California. He then resold the pans to forty-niners for eight to ten dollars each. Before the end of the gold rush, Brannan became a millionaire.

New arrivals at the fields learned immediately that gold mining is hard work.

Among the forty-niners the most popular method of mining gold dust was by using the wash pan. It looked like a pie plate and was usually made of tin or iron. The miner filled his wash pan with dirt or gravel and held it under water while swirling it gently. Gold is a heavy metal. So the flowing water

would wash the light dirt away and leave the heavier gold dust behind.

To pan for gold dust, a miner had to spend back-breaking hours squatting in an ice-cold stream. His hands were under water most of the time. At the end of a long day, his arms felt numb all the way up to his elbows.

Despite the hard work and sky-high prices, new miners splashed into streams, scooped up gravel, and prayed. A few were lucky. "Eureka! Oh how my heart beat!" wrote one miner after he discovered gold in his pan for the first time. "I sat still and looked at it for some minutes before I touched it."

During the gold rush, men used the phrase "seeing the elephant" to describe the feeling of discovering gold. The phrase came from an old story about a Midwestern farmer who all his life had wanted to see an elephant. Finally, a circus came to town and the farmer hitched up his horses and wagon and rode to see it. He was fascinated by his first sight of an elephant, but his horses panicked. They galloped away, dragging the wagon behind them. The wagon broke loose, tumbled down a hill, and was completely destroyed. "I don't care," said the farmer looking at the wreckage of his wagon. "I've seen the elephant."

"Seeing the elephant" became the most popular words spoken by forty-niners. The story of the farmer summed up why they had joined the gold rush. They were willing to risk their health, their money, and their lives for the thrill of finding gold.

One of those who hoped to "see the elephant" was John Augustus Sutter. His 50,000 acres were now crawling with miners. They had trampled his crops, muddied his streams, and slaughtered his cattle for food. "The country swarmed with lawless men," Sutter later wrote. "Talking with them did no good. I was alone and there was no law."

Since he could not fight the waves of miners, Sutter decided to join them. Forgetting his dreams of an empire, he bought mining gear and set out for the hills. His Indian friends told him that gold was bad medicine. They claimed the gold belonged to a demon who lived far away in the hills and would put a curse on those who took the gold away. Sutter dismissed those warnings as Indian superstition.

Often forty-niners found gold in the form of nuggets. Nuggets are a miner's dream. They are lumps of gold that can be as large as marbles. On rare occasions, huge nuggets were found that weighed ten, twelve, and fourteen pounds. The largest single nugget ever found in the United States was dug out of the California gold fields in the mid-1850s. It was a monster that weighed an undreamed-of one hundred and ninety-five pounds.

A lucky miner could stumble on a nugget practically anywhere. Around the campfires at night, forty-niners loved to tell stories about men chancing upon gold nuggets. In one story a miner sat on a rock cursing his luck because he had not found a speck of gold in a month. In anger the man kicked a stone. Beneath it was a shining gold nugget. Another story told of two miners working together in a narrow canyon. For some reason they got into a fistfight. One miner swung at the other, missed, and hit the canyon wall. A gold nugget fell out. Both miners forgot their fight and began scratching at the wall with their hands. And it was said that near Sacramento a little farm girl found a rock she thought was pretty. She brought it to her mother who wiped it off and discovered it was a seven-pound nugget.

As the gold rush stretched into the 1850s, the richest deposits became mined out. But a man could still find a stream where he could pan enough gold to earn about thirty dollars a day. This was a good wage—even in California where prices were so high.

Miners, however, were greedy. They would pack up and leave if someone told them richer diggings lay upstream.

This readiness to move led to a story told by jokesters who traveled from camp to camp. The storyteller said that a miner had died and gone to heaven. That alone was enough to make the miners laugh. Saint Peter told the miner he could not enter heaven because there were already too many miners there. That made the miners laugh even harder. The miner told Saint Peter, "Don't worry. I'll get those guys out of here." Then the miner shouted, "Big strike in hell! Big strike in hell!" The miners stormed out of heaven and raced to the other place. The first miner then said to Saint Peter, "Maybe I'll go to the other place, too. There might be some truth to that rumor about a big gold strike there."

Miners liked to tell stories about other miners who made fortunes. But the largest fortunes were made by men who never dug for gold at all. Businessmen who came west to trade with miners often were more successful than the miners themselves.

Three men in particular made an enormous amount of money without digging for gold. A twenty-year-old named Philip Armour was one. He came to California believing that beef was more important than gold. Armour opened a butcher shop and sold meat to miners. That small shop later became the biggest supplier of beef in the entire United States. Another of these men was Armour's friend, John Studebaker. Studebaker earned a lot of money making wheelbarrows and selling them to gold seekers. He then went home to Indiana and started a factory that built horse-drawn wagons. Some years later the Studebaker company became a multi-million-dollar automobile manufacturer. Possibly the best known of the three was a man

named Levi Strauss. Strauss arrived in California in 1850. He carried a bag full of strong denim cloth and sold a piece of it to a miner. The miner said he was going to use the cloth to make a pair of pants. That gave Levi Strauss the idea of making pants himself. He did, and started the company that makes the pants the whole world today calls Levis.

Writers and artists also flocked to the gold fields. Some of the painters who came were very good. Others were not. But they all tried their hand at painting camp scenes. The art of photography was only a little more than ten years old at the time, but pioneer photographers took excellent pictures of miners at work and play.

Two writers who became legends in America joined the excitement in California. Bret Harte wrote a classic gold-rush story called "The Luck of Roaring Camp." Harte had a friend named Samuel Clemens. The world remembers Clemens by his pen name—Mark Twain. He wrote the beloved books *Tom Sawyer* and *Huckleberry Finn*. Twain also wrote a book about his experiences in mining camps. It was called *Roughing It*. In one chapter, Twain told how he had made the same mistake that thousands of beginning miners had made before him. He found mica, or "fool's gold," and thought it was the real thing. Twain described his disappointment when an old-timer told him he had not found gold:

So vanished my dream. So melted my wealth away. So toppled my airy castle to the earth and left me stricken and forlorn.

Moralizing, I observed, then, that "all that glitters is not gold."

Many different sorts of men swarmed to the gold fields. But women did not arrive in large numbers until the 1850s. Before women began to arrive, men outnumbered women in California twelve to one.

A few women tried to mine gold. But most discovered they could make more money working as entertainers in theaters and dance halls. One entertainer was a singer and dancer named Lola Montez. Her skills in singing and dancing were plain awful, but women-starved miners paid twenty dollars a ticket to see her anyway. After a few terrible performances, Lola decided to retire from the stage and teach singing. One of her pupils was an eight-year-old red-haired California girl named Lotta Crabtree. Overnight, little Lotta became the most beloved child star in the West. She sang with such sweetness that she moved even the toughest miners to tears. When Lotta took her bows after finishing an act, the wildly applauding miners showered the stage with dollars, nuggets, and sacks of gold dust. Lotta Crabtree later starred in theaters in New York, Washington, London, and Paris.

Throughout the 1850s the spell of gold brought more and more people to the territory of California. In 1848, some 14,000 settlers lived in California. Within six years the population had zoomed to a quarter of a million. Only two years after the find at Sutter's Mill, California entered the Union as America's thirty-first state. It was already one of the richest states in the Union, and proudly called itself the "Golden State."

The growth of California's cities was just as dazzling. Sacramento did not exist in 1848. A year later it was a busy town of 12,000 people. And no city in the world ever grew faster than San Francisco.

Before the gold rush, San Francisco was a tiny fort of four hundred settlers. In two years the population soared to 25,000. Thirty new houses were hammered together each day in the booming city. Streets spread over fields where cows had grazed peacefully only a few weeks earlier. The city grew so fast that it even expanded out to sea. Hundreds of ships docking at San Francisco had been abandoned. Their crews had jumped over the side to join the crush of gold seekers. For years those deserted ships rested at anchor. Then land-fill projects pushed into the bay and buried the ships. Even today, ships abandoned during the great gold rush lie rotting underneath San Francisco's streets.

The Great California Gold Rush lasted about a half dozen furious years. By 1855 it had ended. There was still gold in the hills of California, but now expensive equipment was needed to get it out. Gone were the days when a man could pan alone in a stream and find a thousand dollars in gold.

The rich California deposits had made a few men instant millionaires. But for every one millionaire, those same gold fields produced a thousand broken men. They had gambled their lives on making a fortune and had lost.

In San Francisco and Sacramento, the unlucky many gathered in cheap bars. There they sang a song written by a dejected forty-niner:

I lived down in Maine where I heard about the diggins.
So I shipped on a barque commanded by Joe Higgins.
I sold my farm, and from my wife and kids departed.
And to California sailed and left 'em broken-hearted.
Oh, I'm a used-up man, a perfect used-up man.
And if I ever get home again, I'll stay there if I can.

Certainly a used-up man was John Augustus Sutter. He had seen his land ruined by gold-hungry miners. By the time he decided to try mining, he was unlucky and too late. Even though he was there before the gold rush started, luckless John Sutter found no gold. Later he went to Washington, D.C. He appealed to Congress to pay him for the land that had been destroyed by gold seekers. While Congress was considering his request, John Sutter died in a Washington hotel room, another tragic victim of the Great California Gold Rush.

Not all unlucky miners let the disappointment of not finding gold destroy them. Many believed that the experience of participating in the gold rush was reward enough. It was an adventure they would remember for the rest of their lives. After all, they had been lucky enough to see some of the most beautiful land on earth—California.

Other men would never quite get over the thrill of "seeing the elephant." They became addicted to gold mining and dashed to far-off corners of the world at the very hint of a new gold strike. News reached the California fields of strikes in Australia, British Columbia, Nevada, Colorado, and the Black Hills in Dakota Territory. As those incurable miners left California to chase after another dream, they sang:

> Farewell, Old California.
> I'm going far away.
> Where gold is found more plenty.
> In larger lumps they say.